GEMS FOR KIDS

GEMS FOR KIDS

A JUNIOR SCIENTIST'S GUIDE
to Mineral Crystals and Other Natural Treasures

JUNIOR SCIENTISTS

LEE HALL AND ASHLEY HALL

callisto publishing
an imprint of Sourcebooks

To Lee's parents, who helped him collect rocks and said, "Go for it!" when he decided to be a paleontologist. Thank you, always.

Illustrations © Bruce Rankin, 2020. Photographs © halock/iStock, cover; photo-world/Shutterstock, p. ii; J. Palys/Shutterstock, pp. vi, vii; SPL/Science Source, pp. viii, 1, 6; Mark A. Schneider/Science Source, p. 2; Susan E. Degginger/Alamy, p. 2; Deagastini/Science Source, p. 2; Dorling Kindersley ltd/Alamy, p. 10; Nataliya Nikonova/Alamy, p. 10; Derek Anderson/Alamy, pp. 10, 11; Nika Lerman/Alamy, pp. 10, 11; iStock, pp. 10, 11, 25; Shutterstock, pp. 10, 11, 26, 27, 29, 30, 35, 38, 41, 42, 43, 44, 45, 46, 47, 50, 51, 53; Dorling Kindersley ltd/Alamy, p. 11; Fabrizio Troiani/Alamy, p. 11; Jewellery specialist/Alamy, p. 11; Pillyphotos/Alamy, p. 11; Bjorn Wylezich/Alamy, p.13; vvoe/Shutterstock, p. 14; The National History Museum/Science Source, p. 15; hjochen/Shutterstock, p. 16; Panther Media GmbH/Alamy, p. 16; Joel E. Arem/Science Source, p. 17; Haluk Köhserli/iStock, pp. 20, 21; Alfio Scisetti/Alamy p. 28; Ted M. Kinsman/Science Source, p. 31; Dorling Kindersly/Science Source, p. 34; Bjorn Wylezich/Alamy, p. 36; lapidaries/123RF, p. 37; Mark Johnson/Alamy, p. 39; Matteo Chinellato/Alamy, p. 39; rep0rter/iStock, p. 40; igordabari/Alamy, p. 48; The Natural History Museum/Alamy, p. 49; avagyanlevon/iStock, p. 52; Michael Burrell/Alamy, pp. 11, 54; Wojciech Tchorzewski/Alamy, p. 55
Interior and Cover Designer: Heather Krakora
Photo Art Director/Art Manager: Tom Hood
Associate Editor: Maxine Marshall
Production Editor: Ashley Polikoff

Published by Callisto Publishing LLC C/O Sourcebooks LLC
P.O. Box 4410, Naperville, Illinois 60567-4410
(630) 961-3900
callistopublishing.com

This product conforms to all applicable CPSC and CPSIA standards.

Source of Production: Wing King Tong Paper Products Co.Ltd. Shenzhen, Guangdong Province, China
Date of Production: April 2026
Run Number: 5065469

Printed and bound in China
WKT 2

CONTENTS

WELCOME, JUNIOR SCIENTIST! vii

PART ONE:
WHAT IS A GEM? 1

Rocks, Minerals, Gems—Oh My! 2

SO MANY LAYERS 2

ROCKS VS. MINERALS 4

GEMS 8

Types of Gems 12

INORGANIC GEMS 12

ORGANIC GEMS 15

Where in the World Are Gems Found? 18

PART TWO:
THE GLIMMERING WORLD OF GEMS 21

Gem Properties 22
Agate 25
Amethyst 26
Citrine 28
Rock Crystal 29
Tiger's Eye 30
Opal 34
Moonstone 35
Lapis Lazuli 36
Aquamarine 37
Emerald 38
Almandine 40
Grossular 41
Pyrope 42
Peridot 43
Topaz 44
Tanzanite 45
Tourmaline 46
Obsidian 47
Turquoise 48
Alexandrite 49
Ruby 50
Sapphire 51
Diamond 52
Amber 53
Pearl 54

GLOSSARY 58

MORE TO DISCOVER 61

INDEX 62

WELCOME, JUNIOR SCIENTIST!

We are Lee and Ashley, and we are geoscientists—people who study Earth! Just like you, we love gems. But what do the stones that glitter on rings and necklaces have to do with dusty old rocks? As it turns out—everything! Gemstones form inside Earth. Some grow in red-hot magma inside the planet, while others, like pearls and amber, are made by animals or plants. The amazing minerals and rocks that humans turn into gems are the results of **geology** in action. The same physical and chemical processes that create rubies, diamonds, and sapphires also cause earthquakes and volcanoes. Are you ready to become a gem expert? Let's go on a journey inside Earth and learn how our planet makes gemstones!

PART ONE

WHAT IS A GEM?

Let's explore where gemstones come from: rocks and minerals! No matter where you live, there are rocks under you. Buildings, roads, forests, and even oceans have rocks beneath them. Where do those rocks come from? And what about the minerals in rocks that make gems? Taking a closer look will help us understand how gemstones are made.

Rocks, Minerals, Gems—Oh My!

You've already started reading about rocks, minerals, and gems. But what is the difference between them? In order to understand rocks, minerals, and gems, we first need to understand planet Earth.

Gems like aquamarine are valuable because of their beautiful colors.

The rock called pegmatite is made from minerals that grew in hot magma inside Earth.

Minerals like beryl are the building blocks of rocks.

SO MANY LAYERS

Have you ever wondered what is deep inside our planet? The ground under your feet is solid because you live on Earth's hard outer skin called the **crust**. The crust contains the land you can see and touch. It is formed from gigantic slabs of rock. From valleys to volcanoes, and even beneath the ocean, there is crustal rock. However, the crust is just the outer shell of the planet! The entire Earth is nearly 8,000 miles across, and the crust is only 50 miles of that. It would take five and a half days driving nonstop at highway speed to go through Earth from the North Pole to the South

Pole, and you would only be driving through crust for a few minutes on each side! So, what's all the other "stuff" inside Earth? (Hint: It's not a chewy center!)

Earth has five main layers: crust, upper mantle, lower mantle, outer core, and inner core. Imagine driving down to the center of the planet in a car. Can you envision cruising past the crust's glittering minerals and glowing orange magma chambers? After you made it through the crust, you would reach the next layer, called the **mantle**.

The mantle makes up most of the planet. It is hot, dense rock that is pliable because of the extreme heat inside Earth. The upper mantle is about 400 miles thick. The crust and upper mantle are broken into many fragments called **tectonic plates**. There are seven gigantic plates, and many smaller plates, which all fit together like huge puzzle pieces. Rising heat from inside the planet is always moving and pushing them around. The plates may grind past each other, causing earthquakes; dive beneath each other, causing volcanos; or even crash head-on, causing mountains to form!

The lower mantle is Earth's thickest layer. It is 1,400 miles thick from top to bottom. That's as far as the distance from Washington, DC, to the Rocky Mountains (a 22-hour drive)!

At the center of our planet is a metal **core** with an inner and an outer layer. Made of iron and nickel, Earth's core has a chemistry very similar to meteorites. The outer core is 1,300 miles thick and is so hot that it is liquid. Finally, at the

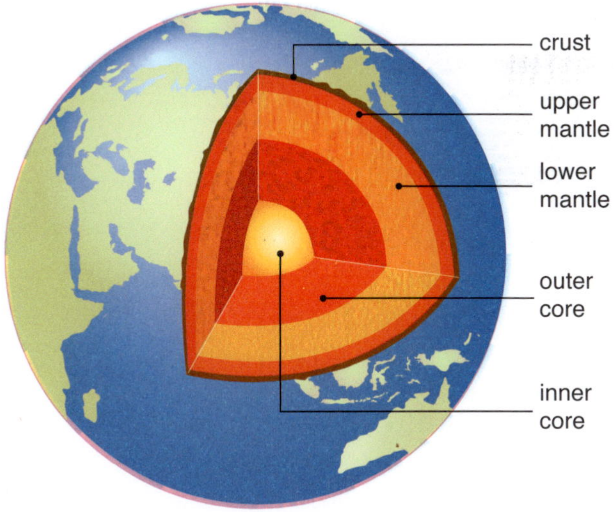

very center of Earth is the solid inner core. The inner core is a giant ball. It is almost 1,600 miles across (that's about two thirds of the size of the Moon!) and over 9,000 degrees Fahrenheit, which is nearly as hot as the surface of the Sun. The pressure at the center of Earth is so intense that it keeps the inner core from melting!

Pyrite is a mineral.

ROCKS VS. MINERALS

Asteroids! Comets! Planets! The universe is full of rocks! From Mars to our moon, to our own planet Earth, rocks are everywhere around you. You can find rocks in parking lots, on beaches, and in your yard. In fact, many buildings are made of rocks. Rocks can be tiny or as big as a house and come in almost every shape and color. But what exactly is a rock?

Rocks are made of **minerals**. Minerals form inside Earth, are made of elements like iron and silicon, and can grow in beautiful crystals.

YOUR MINERALS

Minerals are the building blocks of rocks, but there are also minerals in your body! Ever hear someone say, "You've got rocks in your head"? It's a silly joke, but there actually are tiny rocks in everyone's heads! Otoconia (OH-toe-CONE-ee-ah) are small mineral crystals in your ears that help you balance. Or, maybe you have heard that drinking milk is good for your bones. It's because your bones contain the calcium-rich mineral hydroxyapatite (HI-drox-ee-APP-uh-tyte), and milk is full of calcium! Every bone and tooth in your body contains biominerals, which are minerals grown by a living thing.

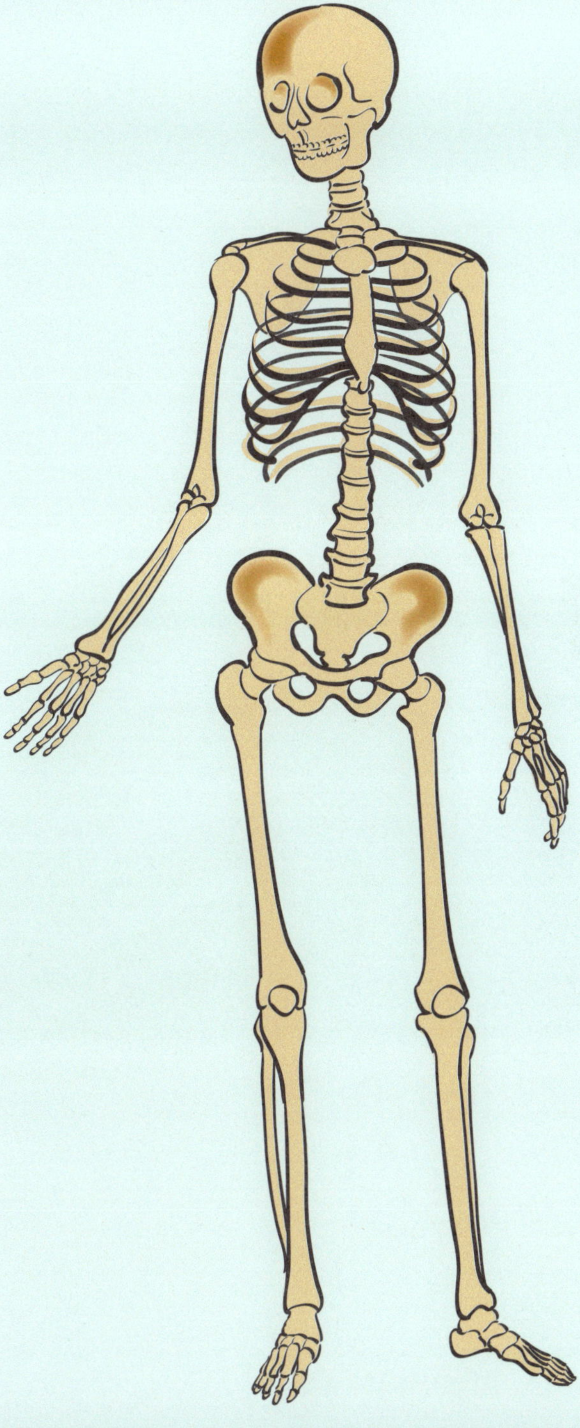

Rocks and minerals are both **inorganic**, which means they are not alive, and they are formed by natural processes. But how can you tell the difference between them? Let's imagine a chocolate chip cookie, for example. Minerals are the ingredients of a rock. Just like flour, sugar, and chocolate chips are ingredients in a cookie, minerals like quartz, feldspar, and olivine are a few of the ingredients that can be found inside of rocks.

Gneiss is a rock.

There are three main groups of rocks on Earth: igneous (IG-nee-us), sedimentary (seh-duh-MEN-tar-ee), and metamorphic (meh-tuh-MORE-fick). These rocks form through the **rock cycle**—a series of natural processes that create, transform, and recycle rocks on our planet.

Igneous rocks are made directly from molten rock, or **magma**, from inside Earth. Molten rock is so hot that it glows bright orange! If rocks are like cookies, magma is like cookie dough. It is soft and mushy and contains all the mineral ingredients needed to make a rock. The minerals will be different depending on where the magma comes from (kind of like a recipe). You would not want to eat this dough, though. It's hot enough to melt your spoon! Just like cookies, igneous rocks must be taken out of the oven—Earth's mantle—to cool down and become solid. When magma erupts out of a volcano, it becomes **lava**. If you've ever seen a video of volcanic lava, you've seen igneous rocks being made! Crystals in lava are usually small because lava cools quickly. The biggest gemstones come from magma that cools slowly beneath the surface, within the crust.

Sedimentary rocks are created when other rocks are broken down into small pieces and then recombined somewhere else on Earth's surface. Rain, snow, ice, and wind break down mountains and hills. This process is called weathering. Water washes the pieces of rocks and soil into streams and rivers where they are tumbled around like clothes in a washing machine. Rocks continue to break apart into smaller pieces until they are washed into lakes or oceans. Sometimes, wind blows tiny pieces of rocks and forms sand dunes. All those tiny pieces of rock, which we call sand, silt, and mud, pile up into layers, like a cake. They are buried under hundreds—even thousands—of feet of more rock . . . a real "rock pile"! All that weight squishes and hardens

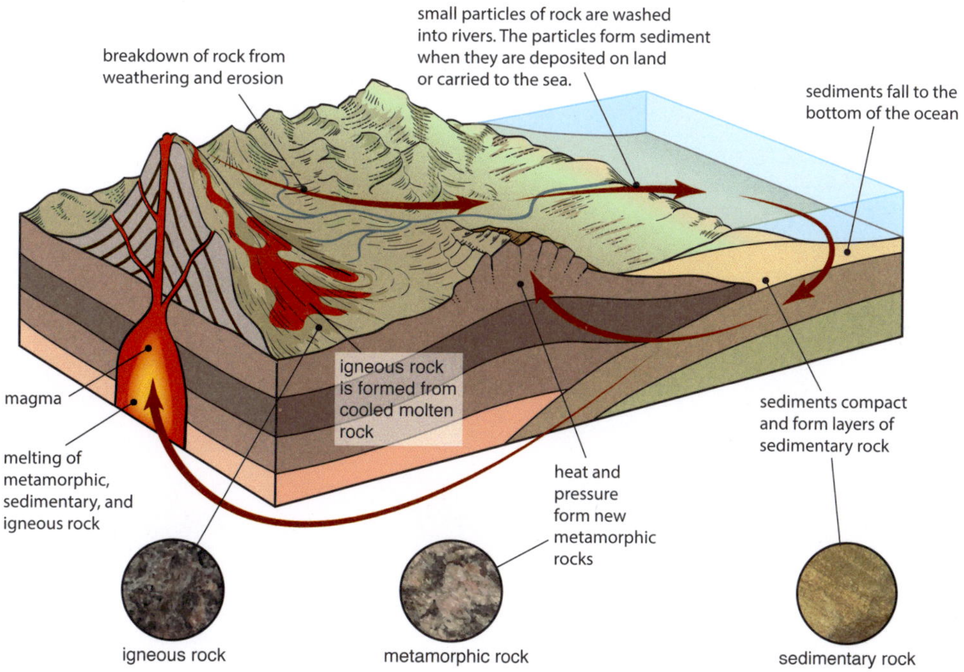

the layers into solid rocks. This is how sedimentary stones like sandstone, siltstone, and mudstone form.

Sometimes, new minerals crystallize inside of sedimentary rocks! Deep underground, hot water leaves behind pure mineral crystals in pockets and cracks in the rock. This is how **geodes** (JEE-ohds), which are hollow rocks with crystals inside, are made.

Metamorphic rocks, the third part of the rock cycle, form when existing rocks get pulled or buried deep underground as the tectonic plates move. These existing rocks could be igneous, sedimentary, and even metamorphic. The rocks are heated to hundreds of degrees Fahrenheit (sometimes they even get hotter than 1,000 degrees!) as they are buried. Unbelievably, these hot rocks squish and fold like taffy and are squeezed by the weight of Earth's crust above. This creates fantastic shapes and folds in the rocks, then recrystallizes them into new rock types like marble, schist (SHIst), slate, and gneiss (NYEss)!

The rock cycle is always in motion around you, constantly working to recycle old rocks into new ones. All three rock types can weather into the particles that make new sedimentary rocks, become buried and heated into new metamorphic rocks, or be melted to form new igneous rocks!

GEMS

You just learned a lot about Earth—way to go! Now you know that minerals and rocks are created in nature, not made by people. You know that different rocks and minerals form depending where on Earth, and where in Earth, you look. You are ready to unlock the dazzling world of gems!

A **gemstone** or **gem** is a natural mineral or other hard material that can be cut and polished so that it looks shiny and beautiful. What do you picture when you think of a gem? Rubies?

Diamonds? Emeralds? These gems are made from mineral crystals. **Crystals** are the solid, geometric shapes that minerals make. People mine uncut crystals from Earth's crust. Gemologists **facet** those crystals to reveal dazzling colors and glittering flashes of light.

Not all gems are minerals, though! Some gems are made from rocks, fossils, or even animal parts (weird, right?).

CORUNDUM

How does one mineral make two different gems? Rubies and sapphires are different varieties of the mineral corundum. Corundum is made from the elements oxygen and aluminum, but sometimes very small amounts of other elements are also found in corundum crystals. If corundum contains the element chromium, it will be red and is known as ruby. If corundum contains iron or titanium, it will have a bluish color and be known as sapphire. Really, it isn't much different from when you make cookie dough and choose to add chocolate chips, butterscotch chips, or white chocolate chips. You bake mostly the same cookies, but the small parts can make a big difference!

BIRTHSTONES

The tradition of birthstones has been around for thousands of years, all around the world. This is the modern American birthstone list. Some months have more than one stone. What month is your birthday in? Can you find your birthstone?

JANUARY

Garnet

FEBRUARY

Amethyst

MARCH

Aquamarine

Bloodstone

APRIL

Diamond

MAY

Emerald

JUNE

Pearl

Moonstone

Alexandrite

JULY

Ruby

AUGUST

Peridot

Spinel

SEPTEMBER

Sapphire

OCTOBER

Opal

Tourmaline

NOVEMBER

Topaz

Citrine

DECEMBER

Turquoise

Zircon

Tanzanite

Types of Gems

Most gems are natural materials that are polished to create colorful stones used in jewelry or decoration. Let's explore the different kinds of gems!

INORGANIC GEMS

Gemstones are divided into two categories: **inorganic** gems (created inside Earth) and **organic** gems (created by the activities of plants and animals). When you think of a gemstone, you probably think of an inorganic gem—a cut and polished mineral crystal like a sapphire or amethyst. As you're about to learn, there is much more to gemstones than meets the eye!

Deep within Earth there are new minerals growing and crystallizing in cooling magma right now. Minerals are made of combinations of different **atoms**. Atoms are the tiny building blocks that make up all the stuff you can see and touch in the universe. An **element** is a substance that is made entirely from one type of atom. If the universe were a toy building set, elements would be the different building pieces. After you make a building, you could take it apart, down to a pile of bricks. You could use the instruction book to rebuild the building the same way it was before, but you could also imagine your own instructions to build other things. Earth does the same thing with the elements in the crust and mantle when rocks go through the rock cycle.

Combinations of atoms are called **molecules**, and a material made up of molecules with two or more elements is called a **compound**. Every mineral has a unique **chemical formula** (the recipe of elements that make up that mineral) that determines how its atoms stick together. The shape, size, and color of crystals are all the result of the recipe of elements and the environments where the minerals grow. Crystals can take thousands, even millions, of years to grow large enough to make gemstones.

Mineral gems grow in many different places. The different depths and temperatures within Earth are like instruction books that tell the elements how they can combine to form different minerals. Some, like feldspar, grow in the liquid crystal mush (like a molten rock slushy) of magma chambers. Others, like garnet, are created when buried shale rocks are squished and heated inside Earth. And others, like corundum (which makes sapphires and rubies), are made when tectonic plates smash together.

Some gems are created near Earth's surface. Opal is made from the elements silicon, oxygen, and hydrogen. Although it is solid and made with ingredients similar to quartz, it is not a mineral because it does not have a crystal structure. Instead, tiny balls of silica scatter light into beautiful flashes of

Diamond mineral crystals form from carbon-rich fluids deep inside Earth.

pink, blue, green, and gold color. Obsidian is another gem that does not have a crystal structure and is made from silicon. It is black silica glass formed when erupted lava cools so quickly that no crystals can form.

Gemstones can even come from outer space! The neon green gemstone peridot (PARE-uh-doh) is mined on Earth, but it can also be found in meteorites that have crashed into our planet.

Unakite is created from an igneous rock called granite.

Not all gems are cut from single-mineral crystals. Rock gems come from rocks that have unique colors caused by combinations of minerals. A famous example is lapis lazuli (LA-pis LA-zoo-lee)—a dazzling blue metamorphic rock. Another gemstone, unakite (OO-nah-kyte), has green and pink crystals and is created when granite is transformed by hot water.

CRYSTALS IN YOUR KITCHEN

Right now, there are thousands of shiny mineral crystals in your kitchen. In fact, you eat these crystals every day! Table salt is a mineral called halite (HAY-lite). Halite is an important source of sodium, an element your body needs to stay healthy. An adult could have the equivalent of 50 teaspoons of salt in their body. Use a magnifier to look closely at salt and you will see the grains are all tiny, perfect cubes. These cubes are the natural crystal form of halite. Although it is too soft to make gemstones, salt is more important for your body than any other mineral in this book!

ORGANIC GEMS

Up until now, you have learned about rock and mineral gems that were made by geological processes. There is another group of gems that are made by plants and animals: organic gems! Organic gems are made from the hard parts of a living organism, or when parts of an organism are buried in sedimentary rocks. If this sounds similar to how fossils are made, you are right! Some fossils are used as gemstones, though not all organic gems are fossils.

The most well-known organic gem is pearl. When a rough grain of sand gets inside the shells of oysters and mussels, they make pearls to protect themselves from getting scratched or hurt by the sand. They surround the sand grain with a smooth layer of the mineral aragonite (ah-RAG-oh-NITE), which creates the beautiful **iridescence** (EAR-uh-DES-sens) of pearls. Pearls are found inside living oysters and mussels and can come in many colors, including black.

Oysters and mussels make pearls inside their shells.

Ammonites (AM-oh-nites) were squid-like animals with hard, coiled shells that lived in the oceans during the age of the dinosaurs. The shells of ammonites were made of aragonite—the same mineral that oysters use to make pearls. Some fossils of ammonite shells from North America are so well preserved that the original aragonite is still intact, giving them deep ruby red and brilliant forest green colors. These shells are known as ammolite—a fossil gemstone!

If you've ever climbed a pine tree or decorated a Christmas tree, you might have found your hands coated in sticky resin. Often confused with tree sap, resin is a thick, glue-like material made by pine trees to protect damaged areas on their trunks and branches. Did you know this resin could become a gemstone? Amber is **fossilized** tree resin. It is usually golden yellow but may be brown or orange, too. Amber often contains fragments of plants, whole insects, or even parts of baby dinosaurs!

Another gemstone created by plants is jet. Jet is very dense coal that was created when many dead trees became buried below Earth's surface. These layers of tree coal were squished under high pressure, compressing them and forming the jet used in jewelry.

Discover more about the organic gem amber on page 53!

Shiny, black jet is popular in jewelry.

SYNTHETIC GEMS

Did you know that gemstones can be created in laboratories? Scientists made the first **synthetic** gems over 100 years ago and have invented several ways to grow beautiful crystals. When the right recipe of elements is combined with heat, crystals can grow before your eyes! Diamonds, emeralds, and even rare gem crystals like moissanite (MOY-sen-ite) are grown in labs around the world every day. You may hear them called "artificial" or "imitation," but these gem crystals are as real as those mined from Earth. Synthetic gems are used in jewelry, but they have other uses, too. Synthetic rubies are used in red lasers, and synthetic quartz and sapphires are used to make watches.

Where in the World Are Gems Found?

LEGEND

- Agate
- Alexandrite
- Almandine
- Amber
- Amethyst
- Aquamarine
- Citrine
- Diamond
- Emerald
- Green Grossular
- Lapis Lazuli
- Moonstone
- Obsidian
- Opal
- Pearl
- Peridot
- Pyrope
- Rock Crystal
- Ruby
- Sapphire
- Tanzanite
- Tiger's Eye
- Topaz
- Tourmaline
- Turquoise

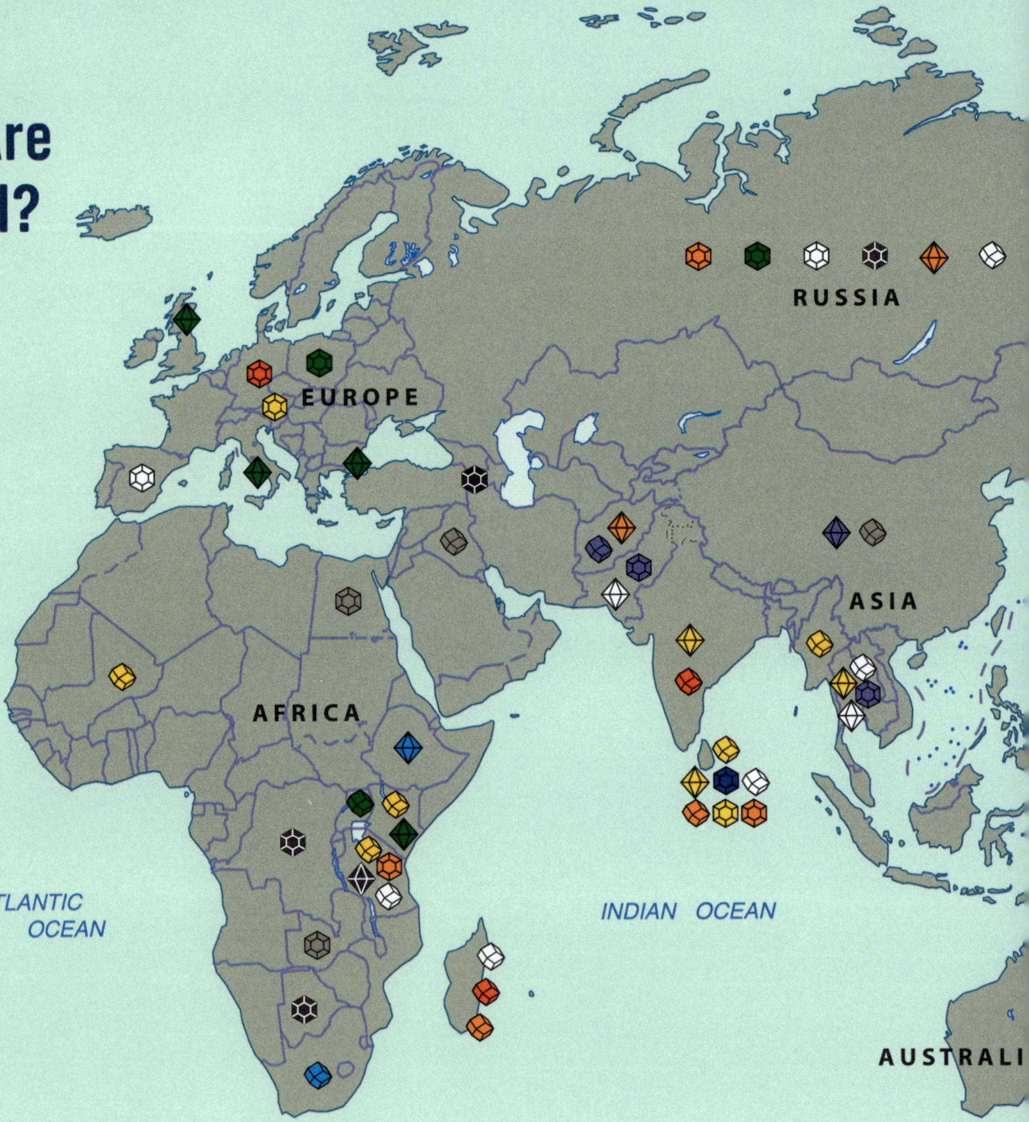

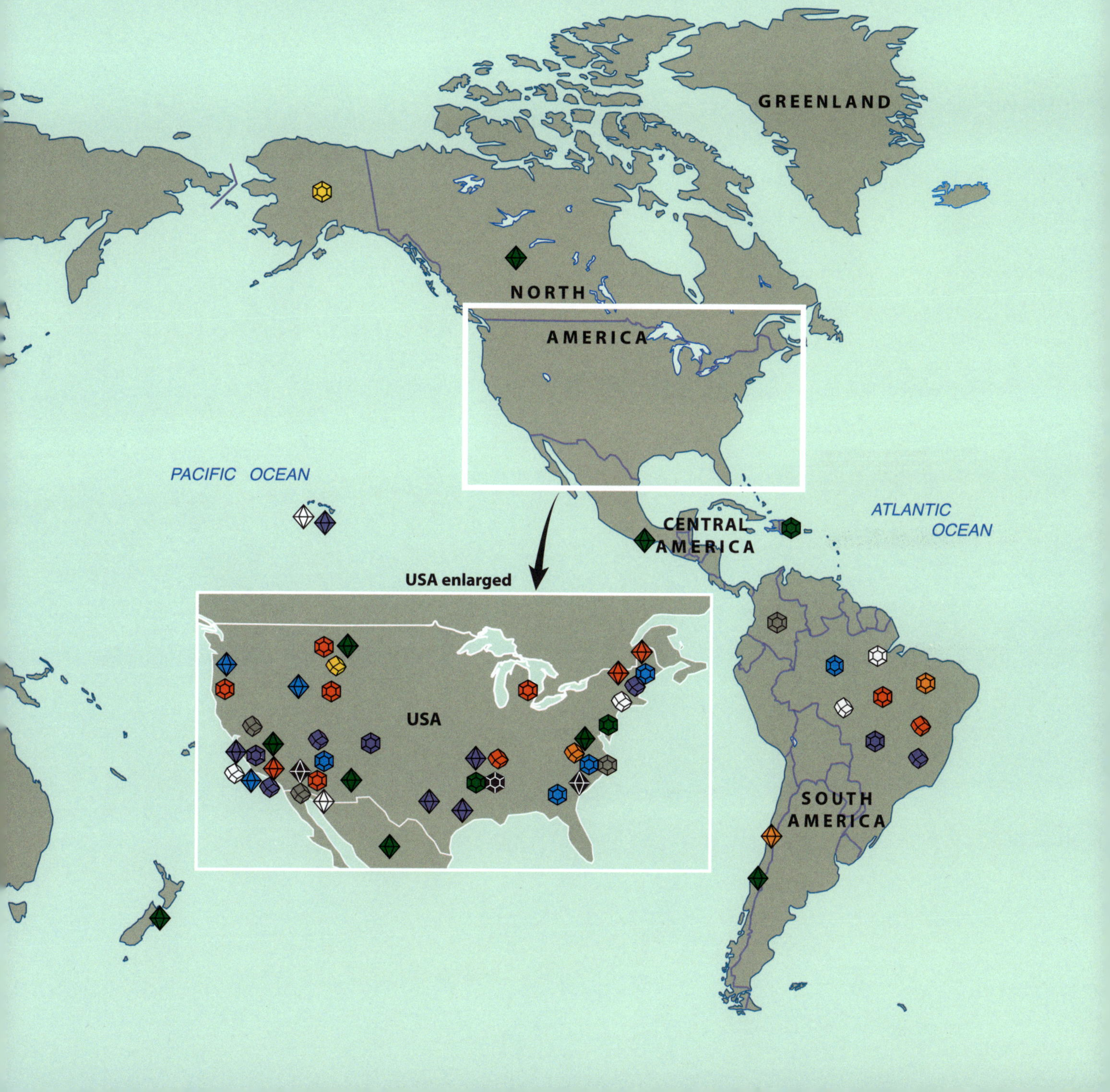
GREENLAND
NORTH
AMERICA
PACIFIC OCEAN
ATLANTIC
OCEAN
CENTRAL
AMERICA
USA enlarged
USA
SOUTH
AMERICA

PART TWO

THE GLIMMERING WORLD OF GEMS

Gems come in many shapes and colors, and more gems are discovered every year. We are going to learn more about 25 of the most well-known gemstones.

Gem Properties

Every gem has different qualities that make it unique. The qualities are called properties. From their colors to their shapes, scientists use gem properties to organize gems into groups. This process is just like sorting laundry. When you put away your clothes, how do you tell the shirts from the underwear from the pants? How do you match up your socks? You use their physical properties! Your clothes have shapes, colors, and sizes that help you sort them. T-shirts are made from light fabric and have short sleeves. Sweaters have thick fabric and long sleeves. Jeans are made of coarse fabric with long tubes for your legs. Gems also have properties that let you organize and identify them. The following properties are used by geologists to identify minerals:

- **Parent mineral:** Sometimes gemstones have names that are different from the minerals they come from. A parent mineral is the name of the mineral type that makes up a gemstone. A good example of this is the mineral quartz. Quartz gemstones include citrine, amethyst, tiger's eye, agate, and rock crystal.
- **Color:** Gem colors are the result of light passing through or reflecting off a crystal and interacting with the molecules that make up that crystal.
- **Hardness:** The hardness of a mineral is ranked on a scale from 1 (softest) to 10 (hardest). The harder the gem, the more it will be able to make scratches on other surfaces. Diamond is the hardest gemstone and is ranked 10 on the **hardness scale**.

- **Luster:** The **luster** of a gem is how shiny or reflective it looks. Lusters can be metallic (shiny like metal) and non-metallic. Non-metallic lusters include clear and highly reflective (like diamond), transparent with a dull sheen (like amber), glass-like (like quartz), translucent with a soft, satiny sheen (like talc), with a wet-looking, oily sheen (like graphite), wax-like with a dull sheen (like chalcedony), muted in color and not transparent or reflective (like chalk), or with a soft, **fibrous** sheen.
- **Cleavage:** When some minerals break, the breaks create smooth surfaces. This is called **cleavage** and is caused by weakness in the mineral's molecular structure. Not all gems have cleavage patterns. There are a few different kinds of cleavage: perfect (clean breaks along smooth lines); imperfect/good (recognizable lines of breaking, but not perfectly smooth or clean); or indistinct/poor (breaks along rough lines).
- **Streak:** The **streak** of a gem is the color that the mineral leaves behind when it is rubbed across a piece of unglazed white porcelain. Some minerals are similar colors but leave different-colored streaks. Some minerals are harder than the porcelain and will not leave any streak.

With adult permission and supervision, you can test the streak of a gemstone by rubbing it on the rim on the bottom of a white coffee mug!

- **Fracture:** When a mineral has no cleavage, we can instead identify its irregular breakage pattern or **fracture**. Examples of possible fracture are **conchoidal** (smooth, ripple-like ridges), splintery (long, sharp points), and uneven (irregular, rough surface).

- **Crystal habit:** The **crystal habit** of a mineral is the shape of its crystals. The shape of a mineral crystal is defined by how its atoms are arranged and also by the environment where the crystal was made. These forms can be **dodecahedral** (with 12 faces), fibrous (like strands of string), **prismatic** (with long, straight sides like a pyramid), **tabular** (like a book or tablet), or many other possibilities.

- **Chemical formula:** The chemical formula of a mineral is the recipe of elements that makes each mineral.

- **Mineral group:** Mineral groups are types of minerals that have very similar chemical formulas and have very similar crystal habits. Minerals within the same group have only very small differences, usually in color. The gems in this book are listed by their mineral group, then by their parent mineral.

Agate

SAY IT! *AG-ett*

Agate is made of the mineral chalcedony (kal-SED-oh-nee), a form of quartz with crystals too tiny to see without a microscope. Agates grow in circular layers inside pockets in volcanic rocks. Hot fluid seeps into openings in rocks and coats them with colorful layers. The layers, or bands, are often different colors because of unique elements in each layer. Did you know wood can be fossilized as gemstones? The petrified (PET-riff-eyed) wood found in Arizona's Petrified Forest National Park are fossils made of agate.

GEM FACTS

PARENT MINERAL: quartz

COLOR: banded red, white, blue, black, or brownish-green

HARDNESS: 6.5–7.0

LUSTER: wax-like with a dull sheen or glass-like

CLEAVAGE: none

STREAK: white

FRACTURE: uneven

CRYSTAL HABIT: no crystal structure

CHEMICAL FORMULA: SiO_2

MINERAL GROUP: silicates

Amethyst

SAY IT! *AM-eh-thist*

Amethyst is purple quartz. The color is caused by iron in the crystals that have been cooked by natural radiation in the rocks around them. Amethyst forms in gas pockets in igneous rocks,. When minerals crystalize inside these hollow spaces, geodes form. Some geodes can be enormous! Tall amethyst geodes, called cathedrals, can be over 20 feet high. Ancient Greeks made cups from amethyst, and Medieval European royalty wore amethyst jewelry as a status symbol.

GEM FACTS

PARENT MINERAL: quartz

COLOR: purple

HARDNESS: 7

LUSTER: glass-like

CLEAVAGE: none

STREAK: white

FRACTURE: conchoidal

CRYSTAL HABIT: hexagonal prismatic with pointed tips

CHEMICAL FORMULA: SiO_2

MINERAL GROUP: silicates

GEODES

Geodes are round stones with plain-looking outsides. But their hollow insides are lined with beautiful crystals! These hollow pockets in stone can be caused by gas bubbles trapped in igneous rock (kind of like a burp) or by erosion of sedimentary rocks. Fluids carry elements like silicon and oxygen into these pockets, causing crystals to grow on the walls of the stone. Quartz geodes are very common and may contain gem varieties like amethyst. Other common geode minerals are calcite and fluorite. Geodes are found in the deserts of the American west, especially California, Nevada, and Utah. If you're not headed that way anytime soon, you can see geodes at your local museum, or buy them at rock and mineral shops or online. Some shops even let you break open your own geodes. Just be sure to wear your safety glasses!

Citrine

SAY IT! *SIH-treen*

Citrine is the rarest quartz gemstone found in nature. The cause of citrine's yellow or orange color is not fully understood by geologists yet, but they do know it is partly caused by radiation affecting iron in the crystals. Most of the world's natural citrine is found in Brazil, but a lot of the citrine available for sale is not natural. It is either amethyst or smoky quartz crystals that have been heated at very high temperatures to turn them from purple or gray to yellow.

GEM FACTS

PARENT MINERAL: quartz

COLOR: yellow, golden yellow, orange, or amber

HARDNESS: 7

LUSTER: glass-like

CLEAVAGE: none

STREAK: white

FRACTURE: conchoidal

CRYSTAL HABIT: hexagonal prismatic with pointed tips

CHEMICAL FORMULA: SiO_2

MINERAL GROUP: silicates

Rock Crystal

SAY IT! *rahk KRISS-tull*

Rock crystal is what most people imagine when they think of a crystal. It grows as hexagonal (six-sided) prisms with pointed tips. These crystals are almost as clear as glass. Quartz crystals grow slowly, adding a single layer of atoms at a time. It could take millions of years for a large crystal to form! In New York State, rock crystals grow in sedimentary rock like dolomite (DOH-low-mite) with points at both ends and are nicknamed "Herkimer diamonds."

GEM FACTS

PARENT MINERAL: quartz

COLOR: colorless

HARDNESS: 7

LUSTER: glass-like

CLEAVAGE: none

STREAK: white

FRACTURE: conchoidal

CRYSTAL HABIT: hexagonal prismatic with pointed tips

CHEMICAL FORMULA: SiO_2

MINERAL GROUP: silicates

Tiger's Eye

SAY IT! *TY-gurz IY*

Tiger's eye is a crack-filling stone that forms in the metamorphic rock called schist. Instead of a single solid crystal, tiger's eye is made of quartz layered with amphibole (AM-fih-bole) crystals. The mineral stripes in tiger's eye create an effect called chatoyancy (sha-TOY-an-see). It is caused by light reflecting off layers in the stone, creating a bright line that looks like the slit of a cat's eye. Tiger's eye stones are cut into round shapes called **cabochons** (KAB-oh-shawn) to show this effect best.

GEM FACTS

PARENT MINERAL: quartz	**STREAK:** white
COLOR: yellow, brown, amber, or black	**FRACTURE:** conchoidal
HARDNESS: 6.5–7.0	**CRYSTAL HABIT:** fibrous
LUSTER: silky	**CHEMICAL FORMULA:** SiO_2
CLEAVAGE: none	**MINERAL GROUP:** silicates

GROW YOUR OWN CRYSTALS

Inside Earth, mineral crystals can take millions of years to form. Thankfully, you can grow crystals in an afternoon! Your crystal ingredients will be sugar and water instead of elements like silicon or carbon. Heat will be provided by your stove (instead of magma), and a jar will be the environment where your crystals grow.

Ask an adult to help you grow your crystals and be very careful around hot water.

What You'll Need:

- **1 (12-INCH-LONG) PIECE OF STRING**
- **PENCIL OR WOODEN DOWEL**
- **GLASS JAR**
- **3 CUPS WHITE SUGAR**
- **COOKING POT**
- **1 CUP WATER**
- **MIXING SPOON**
- **FOOD COLORING (OPTIONAL)**
- **PAPER TOWEL**

continued

What to Do:

1. Tie the string around the middle of the pencil. Trim your string so that it can hang in the jar without touching the bottom. Wet the string with water and coat it with sugar. These sugar crystals are like seeds that the larger crystals will grow on later. Set aside.

2. Fill the pot with the water, and slowly stir in one spoonful of sugar at a time. The sugar will dissolve as you stir. Continue to add sugar spoonful by spoonful until no more will dissolve.

3. Put the pot on the stovetop and heat it on medium high until the water boils. The extra sugar will dissolve now because hot water can hold more. Carefully add more sugar one spoonful at a time until no more dissolves again. For colored crystals, add a few drops of food coloring.

4. Take the pot off the heat and let it cool for 30 minutes. Pour the sugar water into the jar, and lay the pencil across the top so the string hangs without touching the sides of the jar. Cover the jar loosely with a paper towel.

5. Set the jar somewhere it will not be disturbed and check it every hour. As the water evaporates, sugar crystals will grow on the string! It will take several hours for the crystals to grow larger. Remove any crystals that form on the surface of the sugar water so more will grow on your string.

Opal

SAY IT! *OH-pull*

Opal is made of silica and water. Opal is famous for iridescent flashes of color that appear as the stone is turned in the light. Opal forms when water that carries silica passes through an empty space in a rock and leaves the silica behind. The silica forms tiny spheres that reflect light in vibrant colors. Opal can even replace the minerals in fossils. At Lightning Ridge, Australia, fossils that have been "opal-ized" include dinosaur bones, ammonite shells, and even marine reptile skeletons!

GEM FACTS

PARENT MINERAL: none

COLOR: pearlescent pinks, blues, greens, purples, and oranges

HARDNESS: 6

LUSTER: glass-like

CLEAVAGE: none

STREAK: white

FRACTURE: conchoidal

CRYSTAL HABIT: no crystal structure

CHEMICAL FORMULA: SiO_2 plus water

MINERAL GROUP: silicates

Moonstone

SAY IT! *MOON-stohn*

Moonstone is a gem variety of the mineral orthoclase (OR-theh-klase). Orthoclase grows in igneous rocks like granite. Moonstone is unique for its soft, translucent, "floating" sheen, also seen in opals. This effect is created when a crystal that contains orthoclase and albite feldspar cools slowly in Earth's crust. The two mineral types separate into bands within the single crystal, creating the pale blue glow effect. Because of this beautiful glow, ancient Romans believed moonstone was created by solid rays of moonlight.

GEM FACTS

PARENT MINERAL: orthoclase

COLOR: colorless, white, bluish, or pinkish

HARDNESS: 6.0–6.5

LUSTER: glass-like to translucent with a soft, satiny sheen

CLEAVAGE: perfect

STREAK: white

FRACTURE: conchoidal or uneven

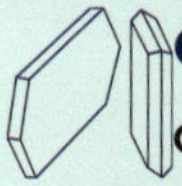

CRYSTAL HABIT: tabular or prismatic

CHEMICAL FORMULA: $KAlSi_3O_8$

MINERAL GROUP: silicates

Lapis Lazuli

SAY IT! *LA-pis LA-zoo-lee*

Lapis lazuli is a metamorphic rock that contains the minerals calcite, sodalite, and lazurite. The blue color of lazurite crystals comes from the element sulfur, the same element that causes the rotten egg smell in spoiled food! Ancient Egyptians powdered lapis lazuli for eyeshadow (used by Pharaoh Cleopatra VII) and used it to color items like the burial mask of Pharaoh Tutankhamun.

GEM FACTS

PARENT MINERAL: lazurite	**STREAK:** bright blue
COLOR: dark blue	**FRACTURE:** conchoidal
HARDNESS: 5.5	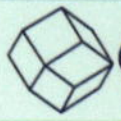 **CRYSTAL HABIT:** dodecahedral
LUSTER: with a wet-looking, oily sheen or glass-like	**CHEMICAL FORMULA:** mainly Ca, Al, Si, and O
CLEAVAGE: imperfect/good	**MINERAL GROUP:** silicates

Aquamarine

SAY IT! *AH-kwuh-mah-REEN*

Aquamarine grows as crystals in igneous rocks called pegmatites (PEG-ma-tytes). Pegmatites have grown some of the largest mineral crystals ever discovered. The largest aquamarine gem, named "Dom Pedro," was discovered in Brazil in 1980. The gem was cut from a crystal three feet long that weighed 100 pounds! Cultures around the world have long loved this gem. Ancient Roman sailors believed aquamarine would protect them at sea, and ancient Egyptians believed it could grant everlasting youth.

GEM FACTS

PARENT MINERAL: beryl

COLOR: blue to greenish blue

HARDNESS: 7.5–8.0

LUSTER: glass-like

CLEAVAGE: indistinct/poor

STREAK: white

FRACTURE: uneven or conchoidal

CRYSTAL HABIT: hexagonal prismatic or tabular

CHEMICAL FORMULA: $Be_3Al_2(SiO_3)_6$

MINERAL GROUP: silicates

Emerald

SAY IT! *EM-ruld*

Emerald is the translucent green form of the mineral beryl. It is closely related to aquamarine, but is deep green instead of blue. The color of emerald is caused by small amounts of the elements chromium or vanadium in the crystal structure. The largest single emerald crystal was discovered in Brazil as part of a large cluster called the Bahia Emerald. The Bahia Emerald weighs over 700 pounds!

GEM FACTS

PARENT MINERAL: beryl

COLOR: green to bluish green

HARDNESS: 7.5–8.0

LUSTER: glass-like

CLEAVAGE: indistinct/poor

STREAK: white

FRACTURE: uneven or conchoidal

CRYSTAL HABIT: hexagonal prismatic or tabular

CHEMICAL FORMULA: $Be_3Al_2(SiO_3)_6$

MINERAL GROUP: silicates

FACETING

Gemstones have different crystal structures, shapes, and colors, so gemologists use different cuts to highlight their unique beauty. Faceting is the art of cutting (grinding and polishing) many small, flat surfaces—also called faces—into gem crystals. When a gemologist cuts all these flat surfaces into a gemstone, it makes the stone more reflective and increases the color and shine of the gem. Faceting requires special tools, and gemologists are very careful not to break the stones while cutting them. There are many different types of gem cuts. One of the most famous is round brilliant, which is the shape you imagine when you think of a diamond on a ring. Another famous type of cut is cabochon, which gives stones flat bottoms and rounded, dome-like tops.

Almandine

SAY IT! *ALL-mun-deen*

Almandine is the most common variety of garnet. Its purplish-red color is the result of the element iron. Almandine has been found in many places around the world and usually occurs in metamorphic rocks called schists and igneous rocks called pegmatites. Although beautiful as a gemstone, almandine is also valued for its hardness. It is crushed to use for grinding and cutting. Paleontology labs use sandboxes full of crushed almandine to hold fossils in place while they are glued together.

GEM FACTS

PARENT MINERAL: garnet	**STREAK:** white
COLOR: deep red to purple or black	**FRACTURE:** conchoidal
HARDNESS: 7.0–7.5	**CRYSTAL HABIT:** dodecahedral
LUSTER: glass-like	**CHEMICAL FORMULA:** $Fe^{2+}{}_3Al_2(SiO_4)_3$
CLEAVAGE: none	**MINERAL GROUP:** silicates

Grossular

SAY IT! *GRAHS-yoo-lurr*

Grossular garnet comes in several amazing colors. It was originally called "cinnamon stone" because it is sometimes brown. Its current name, grossular, comes from the scientific name for the gooseberry plant, which has a green, grape-like berry. The green color of grossular is caused by traces of vanadium or chromium in the crystals. Tsavorite (SAHV-oh-rite) is the most prized form of grossular. It is emerald green and found only in Kenya and Tanzania.

GEM FACTS

PARENT MINERAL: garnet

COLOR: green, cinnamon brown, yellow, or red

HARDNESS: 7.0–7.5

LUSTER: glass-like

CLEAVAGE: none

STREAK: white

FRACTURE: conchoidal

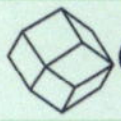**CRYSTAL HABIT:** dodecahedral

CHEMICAL FORMULA: $Ca_3Al_2(SiO_4)_3$

MINERAL GROUP: silicates

Pyrope

SAY IT! *PIE-rohp*

The English name *pyrope* comes from the Latin and Greek words for "fire" and "eye" because of the gem's deep red color and round shape. Pyrope forms in metamorphic rocks, and if it is pure, it is colorless. However, the common red color is caused by small amounts of iron and chromium or vanadium. Sometimes crystals will form that combine pyrope and almandine garnets. These crystals are called star garnets and display **asterism**, a beautiful starlight-like optical effect in the stone.

GEM FACTS

PARENT MINERAL: garnet

COLOR: blood red, cherry red, orange, or colorless

HARDNESS: 7.0–7.5

LUSTER: glass-like

CLEAVAGE: none

STREAK: white

FRACTURE: conchoidal

CRYSTAL HABIT: dodecahedral

CHEMICAL FORMULA: $Mg_3Al_2(SiO_4)_3$

MINERAL GROUP: silicates

Peridot

SAY IT! *PARE-uh-doh*

Peridot crystals form deep in Earth's mantle and are brought to the surface by volcanic activity or tectonic movement. The green color is caused by tiny amounts of iron in the crystal structure. The more iron there is in the crystal, the darker green it will be. Historically, the world's peridot supply came from Zabargad Island, off the coast of Egypt. Peridot is also found in meteorites, but the crystals are too small to make gemstones. Most peridot now comes from Pakistan, Afghanistan, and Myanmar.

GEM FACTS

PARENT MINERAL: olivine (forsterite)	**STREAK:** none
COLOR: green to yellow green	**FRACTURE:** conchoidal
HARDNESS: 6.5–7.0	**CRYSTAL HABIT:** prismatic
LUSTER: glass-like	**CHEMICAL FORMULA:** $(Mg,Fe)_2SiO_4$
CLEAVAGE: indistinct/poor	**MINERAL GROUP:** silicates

Topaz

SAY IT! *TOW-paz*

The biggest topaz crystals are found in pegmatite rock. These can be very large and heavy—over 200 pounds! Small topaz crystals can be found in geodes inside lava. The most valuable topaz comes from Brazil. It is an orange-brown gemstone called "imperial topaz." Topaz crystals are very sensitive to ultraviolet (UV) light from the Sun. If exposed for very long, their colors will fade away!

GEM FACTS

PARENT MINERAL: topaz	**STREAK:** white
COLOR: blue, colorless, light green, or brown	**FRACTURE:** uneven or conchoidal
HARDNESS: 8	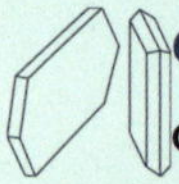 **CRYSTAL HABIT:** tabular or prismatic
LUSTER: glass-like	**CHEMICAL FORMULA:** $Al_2SiO_4(F,OH)_2$
CLEAVAGE: perfect	**MINERAL GROUP:** silicates

Tanzanite

SAY IT! *TAN-zuh-nyte*

Tanzanite is new to the gem world; it was first discovered in 1967 in the Mererani Hills of Tanzania. In fact, tanzanite is found only in Tanzania. It is mined in a small region of metamorphic and igneous rock where marble and gneiss are found together. The rich blue color is caused by the element vanadium. But tanzanite isn't just plain blue. It has a property called pleochroism (PLEE-oh-CROW-izm), which means that, depending on how you look at the gem, it may appear blue, purple, or maroon.

GEM FACTS

PARENT MINERAL: zoisite

COLOR: deep blue or purple

HARDNESS: 6.5–7.0

LUSTER: glass-like

CLEAVAGE: perfect

STREAK: white

FRACTURE: uneven or conchoidal

CRYSTAL HABIT: prismatic

CHEMICAL FORMULA: $Ca_2Al_3(SiO_4)_3(OH)$

MINERAL GROUP: silicates

Tourmaline

SAY IT! *TUR-muh-leen*

Tourmaline has the most color varieties of any gemstone. Ancient Egyptians believed tourmaline came from the center of Earth and received its colors from a rainbow it crossed on the way. But we know today that it forms in rocks like granite and pegmatite, and the different colors are caused by elements like chromium, manganese, and iron. Watermelon tourmaline gets its name because the crystals are pink in the middle and green around the edges (just don't bite them!).

GEM FACTS

PARENT MINERAL: tourmaline

COLOR: red, blue, green, pink, orange, or colorless

HARDNESS: 7.0–7.5

LUSTER: glass-like

CLEAVAGE: indistinct/poor

STREAK: white

FRACTURE: uneven

CRYSTAL HABIT: prismatic

CHEMICAL FORMULA: mainly Na, Mg, Fe, Al, Si, O, and OH

MINERAL GROUP: silicates

Obsidian

SAY IT! *uhb-SID-ee-an*

Obsidian is volcanic glass. It does not have a regular crystal structure like most other gemstones because the lava cooled too fast for crystals to form. Obsidian is black and very shiny. Prehistoric humans used obsidian to make jewelry, tools, and weapons. Obsidian can be chipped into wickedly sharp edges, making it an effective cutting material. It is also dense and heavy. Today, obsidian is used in jewelry and in the music industry. On some record players, the spinning platter that turns the album is made using obsidian. That's a sharp sound!

GEM FACTS

PARENT MINERAL: none

COLOR: black

HARDNESS: 5.0–5.5

LUSTER: glass-like

CLEAVAGE: none

STREAK: white

FRACTURE: conchoidal

CRYSTAL HABIT: no crystal structure

CHEMICAL FORMULA: mainly SiO_2 with Fe and Mg

MINERAL GROUP: silicates/volcanic rock

Turquoise

SAY IT! *TUR-kwoyz*

Turquoise's bright blue color is caused by copper and iron. Turquoise rarely forms as crystals and instead forms as nuggets or veins. It has been used as a gemstone around the world for thousands of years. The name *turquoise* comes from the French word for "Turkish," because it was brought to Europe from traders in Turkey who brought stones from Iran. Turquoise is also abundant in Mexico where the Aztecs called it *chalchihuitl* (chal-cha-WE-tel). The burial mask of Egyptian Pharaoh Tutankhamun has several rows of turquoise in the collar.

GEM FACTS

PARENT MINERAL: turquoise

COLOR: sky blue, bluish-green, or pale green

HARDNESS: 5–6

LUSTER: wax-like with a dull sheen

CLEAVAGE: none

STREAK: white

FRACTURE: conchoidal

CRYSTAL HABIT: no crystal shape

CHEMICAL FORMULA: $CuAl_6(PO_4)_4(OH)_8 \cdot 4H_2O$

MINERAL GROUP: phosphates

Alexandrite

SAY IT! *AH-lex-AN-dryte*

This gemstone is a chameleon! Alexandrite is highly valued for its unique color-changing feature. In natural daylight, alexandrite is green or blue. By the light of a flame, it becomes red or pink! This is called metamerism (MEH-tam-ER-iz-em). Alexandrite forms in metamorphic rocks where silica is not present. Because silicon and oxygen are very common elements on Earth, this is rare. This makes alexandrite one of the most valuable gemstones in the world.

GEM FACTS

PARENT MINERAL: chrysoberyl

COLOR: green, blue, red, pink, or yellow

HARDNESS: 8.5

LUSTER: glass-like

CLEAVAGE: imperfect/good

STREAK: white

FRACTURE: conchoidal or uneven

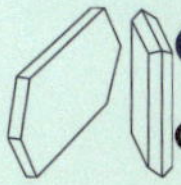

CRYSTAL HABIT: tabular or prismatic

CHEMICAL FORMULA: $BeAl_2O_4$

MINERAL GROUP: oxides

Ruby

SAY IT! *ROO-bee*

Ruby is the red gem form of the mineral corundum. The deep red color of ruby crystals is caused by the element chromium. Some rubies have asterism (see page 42), and show a six-pointed star when cut in a cabochon shape. Because rubies are very hard crystals and easy to grow in labs, they are commonly used as abrasive materials. Abrasives are used for cutting, sanding, or polishing. Take a closer look at a piece of sandpaper and you might be surprised to see thousands of ruby grains!

GEM FACTS

PARENT MINERAL: corundum

COLOR: deep red, pink, or purple

HARDNESS: 9

LUSTER: glass-like

CLEAVAGE: none

STREAK: white

FRACTURE: conchoidal or splintery

CRYSTAL HABIT: prismatic hexagonal or tabular

CHEMICAL FORMULA: Al_2O_3

MINERAL GROUP: oxides

Sapphire

SAY IT! *SA-fire*

Like its sister gem the ruby, sapphire is a form of corundum. Only red corundum is known as ruby. Every other color is called sapphire. Blue is the color most commonly associated with sapphires, though they come in other colors, too. The presence of titanium and iron in the crystal causes the blue color. Most sapphires come from southeast Asia, but a mine in Montana produces gems of pale blue called Yogo sapphires.

GEM FACTS

PARENT MINERAL: corundum

COLOR: blue, purple, yellow, or green

HARDNESS: 9

LUSTER: glass-like

CLEAVAGE: none

STREAK: white

FRACTURE: conchoidal or uneven

CRYSTAL HABIT: hexagonal prismatic or tabular

CHEMICAL FORMULA: Al_2O_3

MINERAL GROUP: oxides

Diamond

SAY IT! *DYE-mund*

Diamond is the hardest of all gemstones, and also one of the simplest, containing only a single element: carbon. After crystallizing over 100 miles deep in Earth's mantle, diamond crystals are rapidly carried into the shallow crust by volcanic eruptions. They are deposited near the surface in igneous rocks called kimberlites (KIM-ber-lytes). Most of Earth's natural diamonds are over one billion years old! Diamonds that aren't gem quality are used for grinding, cutting, and polishing.

GEM FACTS

PARENT MINERAL: diamond

COLOR: colorless, red, orange, yellow, green, blue, or brown

HARDNESS: 10

LUSTER: clear and highly reflective

CLEAVAGE: perfect

STREAK: none

FRACTURE: conchoidal or splintery

CRYSTAL HABIT: octahedral

CHEMICAL FORMULA: C

MINERAL GROUP: native elements

Amber

SAY IT! *AM-burr*

Amber forms when tree resin is buried in sedimentary rock and then hardened. Since amber is created from tree resin, it does not have a crystal shape. Amber is one of the only gemstones that is **fossiliferous** (FAH-sil-IF-er-us). If you look closely at some amber gems, you may see small insects inside! They were trapped in the sticky tree resin before it was buried. The oldest amber discovered is from the Carboniferous period, 320 million years ago!

GEM FACTS

PARENT MINERAL: none

COLOR: golden orange or yellow to brownish-orange

HARDNESS: 2.0–2.5

LUSTER: transparent with a dull sheen

CLEAVAGE: none

STREAK: white

FRACTURE: conchoidal

CRYSTAL HABIT: no crystal structure

CHEMICAL FORMULA: compound of C, H, and O

MINERAL GROUP: organics

Pearl

SAY IT! *PERL*

Pearl is an organic gem that is grown in the soft insides of mollusks, like oysters. Pearls are made of nacre (NAY-ker) and have a soft sheen showing a rainbow of colors. Nacre is made of hexagonal aragonite crystals, the same material that oysters use to grow their shells. Oysters form pearls around grains of sand stuck inside their shells. People can insert a grain of sand into a living oyster to make it grow a pearl. Most pearls available today are created this way and are not from the wild.

GEM FACTS

PARENT MINERAL: aragonite

COLOR: white, pink, dark gray, or black

HARDNESS: 2.5–4.5

LUSTER: translucent with a soft, satiny sheen

CLEAVAGE: none

STREAK: white

FRACTURE: uneven

CRYSTAL HABIT: no crystal structure

CHEMICAL FORMULA: $CaCO_3$

MINERAL GROUP: organics

PROTECTING EARTH'S PLANTS AND ANIMALS

In the past, organic materials like coral, tortoiseshell, and elephant or whale ivory were very popular. These gems were collected by killing living animals without understanding how this would affect their natural populations. The demand for these gem materials caused damage to natural coral habitats and reduced the numbers of animals like sea turtles, whales, and elephants. Today, these animals are among the most endangered life-forms on the planet. That means we could lose them forever. The good news is that they are now protected, and it is illegal to kill and harvest them. As humans, it is important that we understand the effects we have on the world before we take things from nature. This keeps our environment healthy and full of many wonderful, and important, plants and animals!

YOUR VERY OWN GEM COLLECTION

We hope you have enjoyed learning about gemstones—Earth's natural treasures! You now know that gems have histories within Earth that can teach us about incredible geologic forces. Every gemstone, rock, and mineral crystal has a story to tell, and by studying them you can unravel hidden mysteries of geology, space, and time!

Would you like to start your very own rock and mineral collection? It's as easy as picking up stones you find and bringing them home! You can keep them in a shoe box, an old plastic food container, or even a plastic bag. Rinse your stones in the sink and notice how the water helps the colors show up. Use guidebooks and websites to help you identify your finds, and write their names on pieces of paper. Join a local rock and gem club to share and learn more about your discoveries. Before you know it, you will have your very own Museum of Earth. Now you are a certified junior gemologist, so go out and discover your own gemstones!

GLOSSARY

ASTERISM (AS-ter-izm): A star-like optical effect in a gem's crystal, which is revealed when the gem is cut into a cabochon shape

ATOM (AT-uhm): The smallest fundamental building block of all matter, which combines with others to form molecules

CABOCHON (KAB-oh-shawn): A popular gem cut that gives stones flat bottoms and rounded, dome-like tops

CHEMICAL FORMULA (KEH-muh-kl FOR-mu-lah): The recipe of elements that makes up a substance, such as a mineral

CLEAVAGE (KLEE-vuhj): The way in which some crystals break in specific patterns

COMPOUND (kom-POUND): A substance made up of two or more elements

CONCHOIDAL (kon-COY-dull): A fracture type that creates smooth, ripple-like ridges

CORE (kor): The central layer of Earth, divided into a solid inner layer and a liquid outer layer

CRUST (kruhst): The outer layer of Earth, which is exposed at the planet's surface

CRYSTAL (KRI-stl): A solid, geometric shape made by a mineral

CRYSTAL HABIT (KRI-stl HAH-bet): The crystal shape unique to a mineral

DODECAHEDRAL (doh-DEK-ah-HE-dral): Having a ball-like shape with 12 flat sides, which are often pentagons (five-sided) or rhombuses (four-sided)

ELEMENT (EL-eh-ment): A chemical substance that can't be broken down into any other substances and is made entirely of one type of atom

FACET (FA-suht): A small, flat surface cut into a rough gem, or the action of cutting such faces

FIBROUS (FYE-bruss): Resembling fibers or threads

FOSSILIFEROUS (FAH-sill-IF-er-us): Containing fossilized plant or animal remains

FOSSILIZED (FAH-sill-EYEZD): Been changed into a fossil, the petrified remains of ancient plants and animals preserved in Earth's crust

FRACTURE (FRAK-chur): The way a mineral or gem breaks when it does not exhibit cleavage

GEMSTONE (JEM-stohn) or **GEM** (jem): A mineral crystal, rock, or organic material that has been cut and polished to a high shine for use in display or jewelry

GEODE (JEE-ohd): A hollow rock lined on the inside with crystals

GEOLOGY (jee-ALL-oh-JEE): The study of Earth's materials and physical processes including rocks, minerals, plate tectonics, earthquakes, volcanoes, and more

HARDNESS SCALE (HAARD-nuhs skale): A scale from 1 to 10 measuring the hardness of a type of mineral, from softest to hardest; also called the Mohs scale

IGNEOUS ROCK (IG-nee-us rahk): Rock formed when lava or magma cools and hardens

INORGANIC (in-or-GAH-nick): Not created by living things

IRIDESCENCE (EAR-uh-DES-sens): The optical property of a gem or mineral that appears to change colors based on the viewer's perspective or changes in the angle of light

LAVA (LAH-vah): Molten rock above Earth's surface

LUSTER (LUH-stir): How shiny or reflective a gem looks

MAGMA (MAG-muh): Molten rock found below Earth's surface

MANTLE (MAN-tuhl): The middle layer of Earth that contains solid rock hot enough to flow

METAMORPHIC ROCK (meh-tuh-MORE-fick rahk): Rock that has changed into new rock because of high heat and pressure underground

MINERAL (MIN-er-uhl): A naturally occurring, inorganic solid with definite chemical composition and an ordered internal structure

MOLECULE (MALL-eh-kyool): An organized grouping of atoms with unique chemical and physical properties; the basic building block of many crystals

ORGANIC (or-GAH-nick): Created by plants or animals

PRISMATIC (priz-MA-tick): Shaped like a prism with long rectangular sides and the same shape at each end; prismatic crystals can have flat ends or tips that come to a point

ROCK CYCLE (rahk SAI-kl): The never-ending process of rock erosion, burial, melting, and hardening

SEDIMENTARY ROCK (seh-duh-MEN-tar-ee rahk): Rock formed when sediments (small rocks, sand, and minerals) are pressed together

STREAK (streek): The color of a powdered mineral

SYNTHETIC (sin-THEH-tick): Made by humans, not by nature

TABULAR (TAB-yoo-lar): Having flat, thin crystals with short sides similar to a book or tablet

TECTONIC PLATE (tek-TAH-nick plaht): A giant moving piece of Earth's crust

MORE TO DISCOVER

BOOKS

My Book of Rocks and Minerals: Things to Find, Collect, and Treasure
by Devin Dennie
A colorful guide to the wonders of geology including activity pages for the young explorer.

My Awesome Field Guide to Rocks and Minerals: Track and Identify Your Treasures
by Gary Lewis
A handy field guide to the rocks and minerals you will encounter outside your own front door.

WEBSITES

Minerals.net
The best spot for true mineral fans.

Geology.com
For exciting news and facts about geology.

Gemdat.org
To find photographs, maps, and charts all about gemstones.

INDEX

A

Agate
  gem facts, 25
  parent mineral, 22
Albite feldspar, moonstone, 35
Alexandrite
  gem facts, 49
  June birthstone, 11
Almandine
  gem facts, 40
  pyrope and, 42
Aluminum, 9
Amber, 16
  gem facts, 53
  luster, 23
Amethyst, 12, 22
  February birthstone, 10
  gem facts, 26
Ammonite, 15, 34
Amphibole crystals, 30
Aquamarine
  color, 2
  gem facts, 37
  March birthstone, 10
Aragonite, 15, 54
Asterism, 42, 50, 58
Atom, 12, 58

B

Bahia Emerald, 38
Beryl, 2
  aquamarine, 37
  emerald, 38
Birthstones, 10–11
Bloodstone, March birthstone, 10
Books, 61
Brazil, citrine, 28

C

Cabochon, 30, 39, 58
Calcite, geode, 27
Calcium, 5
Cathedrals, amethyst, 26
Chalcedony
  agate, 25
  luster, 23
Chalchihuitl, 48
Chalk, luster, 23
Chatoyancy, 30
Chemical formula, 12, 24, 58
Chromium
  emerald, 38
  grossular, 41
  pyrope, 42
  ruby, 9, 50
  tourmaline, 46
Chrysoberyl, alexandrite, 49
Cinnamon stone, 41
Citrine
  gem facts, 28
  parent mineral, 22
Cleavage, gem property, 23, 58
Cleopatra VII (Pharaoh), 36
Collection, gem, 56
Color, gem property, 22
Compound, 12, 58
Conchoidal, 24, 58
Copper, turquoise, 48
Core, Earth, 3–4, 58
Corundum, 9, 13
  ruby, 50
  sapphire, 51
Crust, Earth, 2, 58
Crystal(s), 9, 13, 58
  grow your own, 31–33
  in kitchen, 14
  synthetic gems, 17
Crystal habit, gem property, 24, 58

D

Dennie, Devin, 61
Diamond
April birthstone, 10
gem facts, 52
hardness, 22
luster, 23
mineral crystals, 13
Dodecahedral, 24, 58
Dolomite, rock crystal, 29
Dom Pedro, aquamarine, 37

E

Earth
core, 3–4
crust, 2
layers of, 2–4
mantle, 3, 6, 43, 52
protecting plants and animals, 55
tectonic plates, 3
Element, 12, 59
Emerald
gem facts, 38
May birthstone, 10
Experiment, growing crystals, 31–33

F

Facet, 9, 59
Faceting, gemstones, 39
Feldspar, 6, 13, 35
Fibrous, 23, 59
Fluorite, geode, 27
Forsterite, peridot, 43
Fossil, 9, 59
agate, 25
almandine, 40
amber, 53
as gemstones, 15–16
opal, 34
Fossiliferous, 53, 59
Fossilized, 16, 25, 59
Fracture, gem property, 24, 59

G

Garnet, 13
almandine, 40
grossular, 41
January birthstone, 10
pyrope, 42
Gem/gemstone(s), 1, 8–9, 59
birthstones by month, 10–11
collecting, 56
faceting, 39
inorganic, 12–14
map of world locations, 18–19
natural mineral, 8–9
organic, 15–16
properties of, 22–24
synthetic, 17
Gemdat.org, 61
Gemologist, 9, 39, 56
Gem properties, 22–24
chemical formula, 24
cleavage, 23
color, 22
crystal habit, 24
fracture, 24
hardness, 22
luster, 23
mineral group, 24
parent mineral, 22
streak, 23
Gemstone. *See* Gem/gemstone(s)
Geode(s), 8, 59
amethyst, 26
description of, 27
quartz, 27
topaz in, 44
Geology, *vii*, 59
Geology.com, 61
Gneiss, 6, 8, 45
Gooseberry plant, 41
Granite, 14, 23, 35, 46
Grinding, 39
Grossular, gem facts, 41

H

Halite, 14
Hardness scale, gem property, 22, 59
Herkimer diamonds, 29
Hydrogen, opal, 13
Hydroxyapatite, 5

I

Igneous rock(s), 6–7, 59
  geodes, 27
  kimberlites, 52
Imperial topaz, 44
Inorganic gems, 6, 12–14, 59
Iridescence, 15, 59
Iron, 4, 9
  almandine, 40
  amethyst, 26
  citrine, 28
  corundum, 9
  Earth's core, 3
  peridot, 43
  pyrope, 42
  sapphire, 51
  tourmaline, 46
  turquoise, 48

J

Jet, 16

K

Kimberlites, diamond, 52

L

Lapis lazuli, 14
  gem facts, 36
Lava, 6, 59
  obsidian, 13, 47
  topaz, 44
  volcanic, 6
Lazurite, lapis lazuli, 36
Lewis, Gary, 61
Luster, gem property, 23, 60

M

Magma, *vii*, 2–3, 6–7, 12–13, 31
  molten rock, 6, 60
Manganese, tourmaline, 46
Mantle, Earth, 3, 6, 43, 52, 60
Marble, 8, 45
Mererani Hills of Tanzania, tanzanite, 45
Metamerism, alexandrite, 49
Metamorphic rock(s), 6, 8, 60
  alexandrite, 49
  almandine, 40
  lapis lazuli, 14, 36
  pyrope, 42
  tanzanite, 45
  tiger's eye, 30
Meteorites, 3, 13, 43
Mineral(s), 4, 60
  building blocks of rocks, 5
  collecting, 56
  rocks vs., 4, 6–8
Mineral group, gem property, 24
Minerals.net, 61
Moissanite, 17
Molecules, 12, 60
Mollusks, pearl, 54
Moonstone
  gem facts, 35
  June birthstone, 11

N

Nacre, pearl, 54
Nickel, Earth's core, 3

O

Obsidian, 13
  gem facts, 47
Olivine, peridot, 43
Opal, 13
  gem facts, 34
  October birthstone, 11
Organic gems, 12, 15–16, 60
Orthoclase, moonstone, 35
Otoconia, 5
Oxygen, 9, 13, 27, 49
Oysters, pearl, 54

P

Paleontology, 40
Parent mineral, gem property, 22
Pearl, 15
  gem facts, 54
  June birthstone, 11
Pegmatite, 2
  almandine, 40
  aquamarine, 37

topaz, 44
tourmaline, 46
Peridot, 13
August birthstone, 11
gem facts, 43
Petrified Forest National Park, Arizona, 25
Petrified wood, 25
Pleochroism, tanzanite, 45
Polishing, 39
Prismatic, 24, 60
Pyrite, 4
Pyrope, gem facts, 42

Q

Quartz, 13, 22
agate, 25
amethyst, 26
citrine, 28
luster, 23
rock crystal, 29
synthetic, 17
tiger's eye, 30

R

Resin, tree, 16, 53
Rock(s), 2
collecting, 56
igneous, 6, 6–7
metamorphic, 6, 8
minerals vs., 4, 6–8
sedimentary, 6, 7–8
Rock crystal, gem facts, 29
Rock cycle, 6, 12, 60
Rubies, 9, 13
gem facts, 50
July birthstone, 11

S

Sapphire, 9, 12, 13, 17
gem facts, 51
September birthstone, 11
Schist, 8, 30, 40
Sedimentary rock(s), 6, 7–8, 60
amber, 53
erosion of, 27
Selenite, luster, 23
Silica, opal, 34
Silicon, 4
alexandrite, 49
geodes, 27
opal, 13
Slate, 8
Spinel, August birthstone, 11
Star garnets, 42
Streak, gem property, 23, 60
Sulfur lapis lazuli, 36
Synthetic gems, 17, 60

T

Table salt, 14
Tabular, 24, 60
Talc, luster, 23
Tanzanite
gem facts, 45
December birthstone, 11
Tectonic plates, 3, 13, 60
Tiger's eye, 22
gem facts, 30
Titanium
corundum, 9
sapphire, 51
Topaz
gem facts, 44
November birthstone, 11
Tourmaline
gem facts, 46
October birthstone, 11
Tree resin, 16, 53
Tsavorite, grossular, 41
Turquoise
gem facts, 48
December birthstone, 11
Tutankhamun (Pharaoh), 36, 48

U

Unakite, 14

V

Vanadium
emerald, 38
grossular, 41
pyrope, 42
tanzanite, 45
Volcanic glass, obsidian, 47

W

Watermelon tourmaline, 46
Weathering, 7
Websites, 61
World map, gem locations, 18–19

Y

Yogo sapphires, 51

Z

Zircon, December birthstone, 11
Zoisite, tanzanite, 45

ABOUT THE AUTHORS

Lee Hall is a paleontologist at the Museum of the Rockies in Bozeman, Montana. Lee has loved geology since childhood. His passion was encouraged by his mother, who would bring him minerals and fossils from rock shops, and by his father, who took him to bookshops and libraries for piles of geology and paleontology books.

Ashley Hall is a paleontologist, naturalist, and science communicator whose passion is teaching everyone about the natural world. She has loved dinosaurs since she was four years old and has spent her career educating kids about paleontology.

Ashley and Lee love hiking, exploring, and their two silly cats.